Ron Proctor

Forgiveness
Fact or Fiction?

Volume 2 - IDENTITY

Copyright © 2018 Ron Proctor
ISBN:978-1-940359-66-3
Library of Congress Control Number: 2018943115
Published in the United States of America

All rights reserved as permitted under the U. S. Copyright Act of 1976. No part of this publication may be reproduced, distributed, or transmitted in any form or by any means, or stored in a database or retrieval system, without the expressed written permission of the author and publisher.

Original Printing
Copyright © 2011 Ron Proctor

Unless otherwise identified, all Scripture quotations are taken from The Holy Bible, New International Version®, NIV®. Copyright © 1973, 1978, 1984, 2011 by Biblica, Inc.™ Used by permission of Zondervan. All rights reserved worldwide. www.zondervan.com The "NIV" and "New International Version" are trademarks registered in the United States Patent and Trademark Office by Biblica, Inc.™

Published by

Bedford, Texas
www.BurkhartBooks.com

Dedication

To my daughter Deborah, son Josh, and daughter-in-law Kelly, these three have been a tremendous help to me over the years.

To my wonderful grandchildren Caroline, Grace, Madelyn, Jacob, Anna Kate, Emma, Levi, and Isaiah, They are the delight of my life.

To Della, my best friend and sweetheart of over 40 years, I would not be the man I am today without my family.

Forgiveness comes about because of the Cross of Jesus Christ. We walk in and pass out our forgiveness because of what happened at Calvary.

Acknowledgments

A special thanks to these people for helping me to put my thoughts onto these pages: Pam Keith, Peggy Ark, and Dr. Don Black.

As I finished this writing I began to think about the different individuals that God had used in my life to help me with the issue of forgiveness. I have decided to take this opportunity to say thank you to those ten men.

William E Bell Jr
Bill Bright
Ron Dunn
David Ferguson
Don Meredith
Bob Sweeley
Chuck Swindoll
Bruce Walker
Jim Walter
Terry Ward

Contents

Dedication
Acknowledgments
Introduction   9

Chapter One: **Walking in the Truth**   11

Chapter Two: **Die to Sin and Live in Righteousness**   27

Chapter Three: **Experiencing Relational Intimacy**   45

Chapter Four: **Applying the Faith Process**   71

Chapter Five: **Stay Dependent on The Holy Spirit**   89

About the Author

INTRODUCTION

For years I let the devil rob me of my joy of forgiveness. Several years ago I experienced a major breakthrough in being free of condemnation.

I have taught my students and over and over again they have asked "put this information into print." Therefore, I have listened and here it is. I hope it helps you as much as the heavenly Father has helped me with the issue of forgiveness. To get the maximum results from this process, read the text first.

This is Volume 2 of the *Forgiveness: Fact or Fiction?* series, entitled *Identity*.

CHAPTER ONE

WALKING IN TRUTH

Who Do You Think You Are?

Hello! My name is Ron and I am a sinner. Can you believe that? I am a Christian; yet I sin. Guess what? I am a forgiven sinner. Who are you? The truth is, you are a sinner too. And if you are a believer, you are also a forgiven sinner. In this chapter, you will learn how to embrace that truth and walk in it.

If you were standing before a crowd of people and asked to give a brief introduction of yourself, what would you say? Who do you think you are? You may associate who you are with an activity or title: "I am a student. I am a wife. I am an athlete." You may answer with your occupation: pastor, teacher, or coach. Part of your answer could be your gender or age. How you see yourself is directly reflected in the answer you give to this question: Who do you think you are? What is your identity in Christ?

When you look in the mirror, what do you see? More than likely, you see your flaws. When you look at your inner self, what do you see? Once again, you probably see your mistakes, your selfishness, and the things you don't feel like you do right. You may see hurt and disappointment or think about bad relationships. When God looks at you, He looks at you in a totally different way. He sees you differently than how you most likely see yourself.

The most powerful truth you can ever learn about yourself is that God looks at you through the lens of the Cross. When He looks at you as a child of His, He sees what Christ did for you on the Cross. You don't have to worry about or try to prove your worth, because when Jesus went to the Cross, He communicated your worth louder than words or works ever could. Your identity in Christ rests on what Jesus accomplished on the Cross, not in your successes or failures.

Consider these verses about your identity and faith:

2 Corinthians 5:21 says:

> *"God made him who had no sin to be sin for us, so that in him we might become the righteousness of God."*

Jesus took our place on the Cross. He took on all our sins. Now we can walk in the righteousness of God.

Hebrews 11:6a says:

> *"But without faith, it is impossible to please God."*

In Hebrews 11 you will find a long list of the illustrious examples of faith. Obviously, these men and women were pleasing to God. They were set apart, given the trophy of being mentioned by name in Scripture, as having walked by faith. It takes faith to please God.

Romans 14:23a says:

> *"Everything that does not come from faith is sin."*

If my circumstances are causing me to trust in things such as finances, people and my own ability, that is sin.

If my emotions cause me to walk in fear, that is sin. If the people around me lead me to walk away from God, that is sin. **Everything, everything is sin if it does not come from faith.**

2 Corinthians 5:7 says:

"We live by faith, not by sight."

Many days things do not go as you planned. Your first reaction may be to throw faith out the window and do things your own way. But God says differently. He says we are to live by faith not by what we see happening around us. He has a plan.

In applying those verses to life, no matter the circumstances, emotions or cultural trends, the believer must walk by faith. And faith is living as though the Bible is true. If you are walking in faith, that changes the way you see yourself.

YOUR IDENITY IN CHRIST MUST BE ROOTED IN UNDERSTANDING THAT YOU ARE FORGIVEN!

The truth is: people are driven by emotion or distracted by the ways the world tries to define us. Insignificant things determine significance. Keeping up with what everyone else is doing or the changing culture often makes a person exhausted. For a Christian, we can operate within the restful rhythm provided by our identity in Christ instead of the confusion of culture which makes us unsure of who we are. In that case, we have looked to the wrong thing to define us: approval of others (horizontally) instead of God's approval (vertically.) So what is the truth?

Four Truths to Consider About Your Identity in Christ

The following four truths will help you to understand your identity in Christ. When the enemy comes to deceive you, when he tries to make you see yourself through his eyes instead of the way God sees you, look to these four truths as you anchor.

Truth #1: Apply the Faith Process

The best way to understand the truth about your identity is to apply the Faith Process to God's Word.

- Review the Faith Definition: Faith is choosing to live as though the Bible is true, regardless of circumstances, emotions or cultural trends. Remember all that you read about faith:

  1. If I am not living by faith, then I am not pleasing God.

  2. If I am not living by faith, then I am living in sin.

  3. I must live by faith, not just by what I can see.

- Ask yourself; "If I were living as though this passage of Scripture were true, then how would I be living?" Use this question to help you apply every Scripture you read. Scripture is there to live by, not just to say we read our devotion or our homework assignment. Make it real in your life.

- Pray for the Holy Spirit's help. You cannot do this alone. At salvation, God gave you the Holy Spirit to guide you. Ask Him for His help in living out what you learn in Scripture.

In every situation, apply the Faith Process. Whenever you encounter a situation in which you struggle to accept and implement how God sees you as a believer in Christ, stop and apply the Faith Process to His Word.

Galatians 2:20 says:

"I have been crucified with Christ and I no longer live, but Christ lives in me. The life I now live in the body, I live by faith in the Son of God, who loved me and gave himself for me."

As a believer, I must surrender all that I am to all that He is. I give up my will to follow His will. If I live out this verse, I will live like Christ. Daily, I must ask the Holy Spirit to help me live the Christian life. We died to sin at the Cross. We are no longer to live for ourselves. Instead, we are to let Jesus Christ live His life through us.

2 Corinthians 5:21 says:

"God made him who had no sin to be sin for us, so that in him we might become the righteousness of God."

Jesus is sinless. Jesus took on our sin at the Cross. We took on the righteousness of God when we became

God's children. We are forgiven! If I am living as though that is true I am living knowing that I am forgiven. What freedom! I can walk in joy and not walk everyday overcome by my condemnations.

Romans 6:11-13 says:

> *"In the same way, count yourselves dead to sin but alive to God in Christ Jesus. Therefore do not let sin reign in your mortal body so that you obey its evil desires. Do not offer any part of yourself to sin as an instrument of wickedness, but rather offer yourselves to God as those who have brought from death to life; and offer every part of yourself to him as an instrument of righteousness."*

Christians need to learn how to get good at dying to themselves! These verses remind you not to let sin control you. Instead, yield yourself to God as one who has been raised from the dead. If I am living by faith, I will give God control and step out of the way. Is that easy? No! That's why you must ask for the Holy Spirit's help. According to these verses, you can wake up each day knowing that because of Jesus's death on the Cross, you do not have to be dominated by sin.

Hebrews 10:10, 14 says:

> *"And by that will, we have been made holy through the sacrifice of the body of Jesus Christ once for all. For by one sacrifice he has made perfect forever those who are being made holy."*

According to verse ten, God made you holy, perfect, forgiven. This verse describes both the grandeur and finality of what God has made you. Because of His sacrifice on the Cross, you are made holy, not because of anything you have done. This truth doesn't function as a discouragement but rather serves as an invitation to rest in what Jesus has accomplished. We have the temptation or tendency to try to earn or prove our holiness. Instead, we can rest in the accomplishment and victory of Christ over sin and death.

FAITH, FACT, FEELING
Faith feeds the facts. Feelings follow.

FACT　　　　　FAITH　　　　FEELINGS

Imagine these words were cars in a train. **FACT** would be the engine, **FAITH** the fuel car, and **FEELINGS** the caboose. As the Christian responds to circumstances, emotions, and cultural trends, sometimes these train cars get off track and out of order. The caboose or feelings try to run ahead of the engine, truth. The truth in God's Word should always overcome the passion aroused by a believer's feelings. God's truth fuels the Christian's faith, which overrules anything else.

You are to live day by day in the process of becoming what you have already been declared. He has made you holy through what Jesus did. You may not feel like you are holy. Remember that truth is not based on feelings but on facts of Scripture. Every day holiness is a process; a marathon, not a sprint. Every day you must wake up and say, "I am forgiven. I will put away sin today. I am holy."

- God has declared you holy. (**Positional Sanctification**)

   "And by that will, we have been made holy through the sacrifice of the body of Jesus Christ once for all."
   Hebrews 10:10

- You are in the process of becoming holy. (**Experiential Sanctification**)

   "For by one sacrifice he has made perfect forever those who are being made holy."
   Hebrews 10:14

- You are waiting for glorification in heaven. (**Ultimate Sanctification**)

   *"See what great love the Father has lavished on us, that we should be called children of God! And that is what we are! The reason the world does not know us is that it did not know him. Dear friends, now we are children of God, and what we will be has not yet been made know. But what we know that when Christ appears, **we shall be like him**, for we shall see him as he is. All who have this hope in him purify themselves, just as he is pure."*
   1 John 3:1-3

You are on a sanctification journey. When you came to know Christ, the journey began. You took on the holiness of God at salvation. (Positional Sanctification) Day by day, the journey continues.

1 Peter 2:9 says:

"But you are a chosen people, a royal priesthood, a holy nation, God's special possession, that you may declare the praise of him who called you out of darkness into his wonderful light."

God declares us a chosen people (Positional Sanctification) to live a life that declares His praises (Experiential Sanctification.) One day in heaven, sanctification will be seen in full as we are made totally perfect in Him. (Ultimate Sanctification)

Truth #2: Understand Your Enemy: Satan

People picture Satan as a guy in a red suit with a pitch fork. But he is deceptive. He may come to you in a three-piece suit driving a shiny car. He doesn't always approach you looking evil. Beware! We must know our enemy. Just as a boxer watches film from a previous match to know what he is up against, we must also be vigilant to know our enemy, so we can be well equipped against him.

- We have an enemy and his name is Satan. John 10:10 gives a vivid description of Satan's intent to kill, steal and destroy our identity with Christ.

- John 8:44 says, that he also tries to lie to us about our identity. He wants you to live thinking you are unforgiven.

How does the devil deceive, kill, steal and destroy? His level of commitment to deceive is directly proportional to how valuable the understanding of your identity in Christ is to your walk with Christ. He is constantly on the attack because there is much at stake. In other words, he is watching to see how your identity in Christ is lining up with your walk with Christ. He uses your performance to defeat you. He whispers in your ear, "You are not doing enough, you are not living up to what God wants, and look what someone else is doing." When he attacks, you must know what your plan is to defeat him.

Truth #3: Practice Biblical Meditation

For each Scripture you read, apply the Faith Process. Meditate on and memorize Scripture. You can't apply the Faith Process without Scripture. This means getting into God's Word daily.

Who Does the Bible Say You are in Christ?

Scripture speaks plainly describing the follower's identity in Christ.

- **I am a child of God.** John 1:12 (NIV): *Yet to all who did receive him, to those who believed in his name, he gave the right to become children of God.*

We are not strangers to God. We are given the right to call ourselves His children: loved and seen by our eternal Father who is God.

- **I am a friend of Jesus.** John 15:15 (NIV): *I no longer call you servants, because a servant does not know his master's business. Instead, I have called you friends, for everything that I learned from my Father I have made known to you.*

Jesus has made known to us the will of his Father and therefore we are considered his friends. Despite our shortcomings and despite the countless ways we fail him, Jesus still chooses to closely associate with us as his friends.

- **I am no longer condemned.** Romans 8:1 (NIV): *Therefore, there is now no condemnation for those who are in Christ Jesus.*

Because we know that condemnation does not come from Jesus, we can therefore understand that it is often used against us. Don't forget that he took our shame and condemnation on the Cross, so we wouldn't have to. In Christ, we are free to walk without condemnation in things past, present and future.

- **I am a fellow heir of Jesus.** Romans 8:17 *Now if we are children, then we are heirs—heirs of God and co-heirs with Christ, if indeed we share in His suffering in order that we may also share in His glory.*

Because we are heirs, we are given the same things he is given, namely: eternal life with the Father. We also share in his sufferings and experience his glory alongside him. For the glory that is His, this is an important aspect of the Christian life: that we commit to taking up our own crosses to share in His sufferings.

- **I am a new creation.** 2 Corinthians 5:17 (NIV): *Therefore, if anyone is in Christ, the new creation has come: The old has gone, the new is here!*

We have died to ourselves; the old desires, the old lusts, the old tendencies and habits have all died along with us. We no longer live to please ourselves, but exist to bring glory to the Father. This is what our new creation celebrates: a life full of worship and adoration to the Father who has made us new!

- **I am no longer a slave to sin.** Galatians 4:7 (NIV): *So you are no longer a slave, but God's child; and since you are his child, God has made you also an heir.*

We were once slaves to sin and darkness, but God purchased us through Jesus on the Cross. Because of Christ's sacrifice, we are given the title of His children and heir to Jesus. The depth of his grace is epitomized at the Cross. We don't deserve either of these titles; yet, they have been made available through Christ!

- **I am God's poem.** Ephesians 2:10 (NIV): *For we are God's handiwork, created in Christ Jesus to do good works, which God prepared in advance for us to do.*

God shows us off as his handiwork! Everything about us is exactly how He designed us, perfect and created to do good works. We are in Christ Jesus, therefore our activity and identity is to be defined by Him! Remember: God sees the believer through the lens of Jesus on the Cross, forgiven. He doesn't see the believer through the filthy lens of sin.

- **I am holy in God's sight.** Hebrews 10:10 (NIV): *And by that will, we have been made holy through the sacrifice of the body of Jesus Christ once for all.*

    Our salvation isn't earned. It was bought and paid for by Christ's sacrifice on the Cross. We are made holy through the sacrifice of and relationship to Christ. The holiness we have because of Christ's sacrifice is given to the Christian once for all and cannot be taken away by things done or not done.

- **I am in the process of becoming holy.** Hebrews 10:14 (NIV): *For by one sacrifice he has made perfect forever those who are being made holy.*

    For those who are in Christ, we are considered perfect because of what Christ did for us. We did nothing! Because of what Christ did, we receive all the benefits. It is through His sacrifice that we become (experientially) what we already are (positionally): HOLY.

- **Jesus is my strength.** John 15:1-5 (NIV): *I am the true vine, and my Father is the gardener. He cuts off every branch in me that bears no fruit, while every branch that does bear fruit he prunes so that it will be even more fruitful. You are already clean because of the word I have spoken to you. Remain in me, as I also remain in you. No branch can bear fruit by itself; it must remain in the vine. Neither can you bear fruit unless you remain in me. I am the vine; you are the branches. If you remain in me and I in you, you will bear much fruit; apart from me you can do nothing.*

    Christians must understand that fighting the battles of this world cannot be done without the Holy Spirit. We must stay connected and draw strength from His help. The verse puts it plainly: without God's help we can do nothing.

- **My body is the dwelling place of God.** 1 Corinthians 6:19-20 (NIV): *Do you not know that your bodies are temples of the Holy Spirit, who is in you, whom you have received from God? You are not your own; you were bought at a price. Therefore honor God with your bodies.*

First, knowing that the Holy Spirit is always there should bring comfort. We have God's own Spirit dwelling in us. It is also a warning. Representing God's Spirit in us, what are we presenting to the world? Honor God.

- **I have taken on the righteousness of God.** 2 Corinthians 5:21 (NIV): *God made him who had no sin to be sin for us, so that in Him we might become the righteousness of God.*

Jesus took my sin to the Cross. By accepting Him as my Savior, I can live each day in forgiveness taking on the righteousness of God.

- **Christ lives in me.** Galatians 2:20 (NIV): *I have been crucified with Christ and I no longer live, but Christ lives in me. The life I now live in the body, I live by faith in the Son of God, who loved me and gave himself for me.*

We died with Christ positionally at the Cross. We no longer live for ourselves. We are to let Jesus Christ live His life through us.

- **I have been blessed with every spiritual blessing.** Ephesians 1:3 (NIV): *Praise be to the God and Father* *of our Lord Jesus Christ, who has blessed us in the heavenly realms with every spiritual blessing in Christ.*

Wow! Every spiritual blessing has been given to every believer. He doesn't bestow those blessing because of what I do or how talented I am. They are given in Christ. Every day we can look for the blessings God has in store and praise Him for them!

- **I have been chosen to be holy and blameless before God.** Ephesians 1:4 (NIV): *For He chose us in him before the creation of the world to be holy and blameless in his sight.*

God created man to be holy. When man chose sin, God made a way for man to be holy. The only way is through Jesus Christ, his son. Now we can be holy and blameless before God.

- **God has chosen me.** 1 Thessalonians 1:4 (NIV): *For we know, brothers and sisters loved by God, that he has chosen you.*

Isn't it a wonderful thought that God chose you? Long before you turned to God, he was already seeking you. He loves you and because of that, you can walk in forgiveness.

- **He's not ashamed of me.** Hebrews 2:11 (NIV): *Both the one who makes people holy and those who are made holy are of the same family. So Jesus is not ashamed to call them brothers and sisters.*

I am adopted into the family of God. Jesus proudly calls me his family.

These verses help you to see who you are in Christ. But you cannot live this life on your own.

Truth #4: Look to the Holy Spirit for Help

Christians are not expected to go through this life alone. Jesus gives us the Holy Spirit to help us. Rely on the Holy Spirit to teach you the truth about your identity, to guide you in understanding your identity and to empower you to live out your identity in Christ. In Chapter 4, you will read more details on how to stay dependent on the Holy Spirit for everyday living.

Let the Bible inform you about who you are, not your circumstances, not your emotions, and certainly not the cultural trends. This will always be in flux, but the Word of God is consistently true, no matter what.

Today, choose to believe that you are holy in God's sight because of the sacrifice of Jesus Christ on the Cross,

**GOD SEES YOU AS HOLY AND FORGIVEN.
AND BECAUSE I AM FORGIVEN,
I CAN FORGIVE OTHERS!
YOU ARE! YOU CAN!**

DIE TO SIN AND LIVE IN RIGHTEOUSNESS

The Cross Changes Everything!

You have probably heard this before but ponder again the meaning of this phrase, "The Cross changes everything." It is no coincidence that this lesson begins by placing this reality at the forefront of our minds. What Jesus did on the Cross is both the crux of the Christian faith and of human history. On the Cross, the ultimate sacrifice was made, the wrath of God was ap-peased, grace was poured out for those who believe and eternal life with God the Father was made possible. If that wasn't enough, along with His sacrifice, came the most important invitation we could ever respond to: die along with Him at salvation (positionally) and remember to continue dying to yourself every day (experientially).

Positional   Experiential   Ultimate

Ron Proctor

Positional	Experiential	Ultimate
Positional Christians have a new identity in Jesus. They belong to God.	Process whereby the indwelling Holy Spirit gradually transforms Christians into the image of Jesus Christ.	Completion of Sanctification when the Christian is conformed completely to the image of Christ when they die.

We can view the Cross as entitlement to what comes after death or we can rightly see it as the most treasured act of love and grace that is worthy of our lifelong worship. When we respond to the Cross with daily dying to our self, we will be much less likely to fall into sin and temptation.

In this lesson we will answer important questions that relate to sin and temptation. By answering these questions properly, we can better understand how we are to approach and handle sin. This understanding will hopefully birth a necessary awareness to both the severity of sin and the importance of an action plan against temptation and sin.

1. What should Christians do with temptation?

2. What should I do as I ponder the possibility of sinning against God?

Every Christian faces temptation every day. We need a plan on how to resist the different temptations we face in life. Galatians 5:16 says:

> *"So I say, walk by the Spirit, and you will not gratify the desires of the flesh."*

> **EVERY DAY:**
>
> 1. We have a choice not to sin
> 2. There is a battle going on within us to sin
> 3. Yield to the Spirit and we will not sin.

When we properly consider what it cost to pay for our sin and how the power to resist sin lives in us, we can answer these questions the right way. No one is born with a theology; therefore, we must rediscover the truth of Scripture for ourselves. We must also strive to join the unchanging, unwavering answer of the Bible to the ever-changing questions of our culture.

Galatians 2:20 says:

"I have been crucified with Christ and I no longer live, but Christ lives in me. The life I now live in the body, I live by faith in the Son of God, who loved me and gave himself for me."

Faith Definition:
Faith is choosing to believe as though the Bible is true regardless of circum-stances, regardless of emotions, and regardless of cultural trends.

We must remember that we have already died to ourselves, giving up the choices and deci-sions that reflect personal gain and glory, to bring Him glory with our whole lives. Under the shadow of the Cross, our sin is taken away and our old selves are invited to die (positionally) along with Jesus. If we choose to believe that the Galatians 2:20 is true, we give up our right to sin (experientially).

Does God have a plan to help us overcome temptation? What does the Bible say about temptation? Should I just give in and not resist temptation?

1 Corinthians 10:13 says:

> *"No temptation has overtaken you except what is common to man-kind. And God is faithful; he will not let you be tempted beyond what you can bear. But when you are tempted, he will also provide a way out so that you can endure it."*

Consider this important phrase that comes from this verse, *"And God is faithful; he will not let you be tempted beyond what you can bear."* The Bible says that God never lies (Hebrews 6:18) and therefore, God will never allow us to be tempted beyond what we can handle. This promise directly collides with what often comes along with temptation: **the misconception that we do not have a choice.** God has made a way for us to overcome sin and it starts with remembering that we have died to sin upon salvation and must continue to die to sin daily.

Paul's Advice for the Temptation Challenge

In Romans 6, Paul gives great advice in dealing with temptation. At the beginning of the chap-ter, he asks a challenging question for every follower of Jesus Christ: "Shall we continue to sin?" His answer is "NO!" Look closely at the following admonishment of Paul regarding the appropriate way to handle temptation: *"We died to sin"* (Romans 6:2). This short but powerful declaration has massive implications for the Christian struggling with temptation and sin. If we have allowed sin to reign in our lives, it means that we are forgetting one of the most important characteristics of our identity in Christ.

In our relationship with Jesus Christ, we die with Him at salvation (positionally) and give up every right to sin. Therefore, if it has any place in our hearts, there must be a disconnect between what we have understood and declared at salvation and what we are doing now in our daily lives. We were not designed to live dualistically, saying one thing and doing another, but rather in total surrender to Jesus, continually fueled by worship and adoration of our Savior. Paul continues his indictment of sin in the remainder of verse 2, *"how can we live in it any longer?"* Paul offers a simpler yet clear approach to sin: it has no place in our lives.

Sin has no place in our lives!
Sin has no place in our lives!

In application of Paul's admonition to stop sinning, Christians must search their hearts for anything that needs confessing, asking the Holy Spirit to bring to light anything that offends God. Sometimes sin remains dormant. If asked, the Holy Spirit will bring them to light and empower you to confess them to God and to a close friend, family member or class mate. Confessing to an individual who can help keep you accountable is healthy. It is important to remember that confession is the act of acknowledging our sin to God, drinking in His lavish grace and responding to His goodness with our repentance and obedience. We will continue to battle with sin each and every day. The better we get at confession, the more likely sin will not grip tightly to our lives. We must get good at bringing our sin out of the darkness and into the light where it cannot live and take hold of us.

New DNA

Romans 6:6 says:

"Our old body of sin was crucified with Christ so that the body of sin might be done away with."

When we came to Christ we were crucified with Christ and we died with Christ. Since we have died with Christ we realize that sin is not part of the DNA of the follower of Christ. Our new DNA is righteousness. Therefore, righteous living is the daily goal of every child of God because we desire to please God with our behavior (experiential righteous).

Romans 6:11 says:
"Count yourselves dead to sin."

Paul exhorts us to get good at dying in this verse. Therefore, this is the responsibility of every child of God that we discover how to get good at dying to our sin every day. This is the only way to resist temptation.

ALWAYS REMEMBER: DEAD PEOPLE DO NOT SIN

Romans 6:12-13 says:

"Therefore do not let sin reign in your mortal body so that you obey its evil desires. Do not offer any part of

yourself to sin as an instrument of wickedness; but rather offer yourselves to God as those who have been brought from death to life, and offer every part of yourself to him as an instrument of righteousness."

Paul's great chapter detailing the battle against sin in the life of the believers gives powerful clues and "how tos" regarding sin. Verses 12 and 13 have both negative and positive commands for us. Paul says *"do not let sin reign"* and *"do not offer any part of yourself to sin as an instrument of wickedness."* He's simply saying that when we allow ourselves to surrender to sin's temptations, we are letting sin rule and reign within us! The present tense of these two negative imperatives reveal what is happening—we keep giving ourselves to sin.

Verse 13, however, also carries the positive command that is our solution. On the one hand, we stop presenting ourselves or making ourselves available to sin, but on the other hand, we ACT in a decisive way to present ourselves to God. This verb is an Aorist Imperative. Since this kind of verb emphasizes punctiliar action more than any other kind of action, we realize Paul is saying **"decisively present yourself to God!"** You must actively give yourselves to God (experiential righteous).

You must actively give yourselves to God!

When you went to the Cross at salvation, Jesus took away the penalty of your sin and gave you the power over your sin. When you received Christ into your life, you took on the identity of Jesus Christ that gave you power over sin. You died with Christ positionally which means He gave you life and You told Him that He could rule in your life (experiential righteous).

Hebrews 12:1-2 says:

> *"Therefore, since we are surrounded by such a great cloud of witnesses, let us throw off everything that hinders and the sin that so easily entangles. And let us run with perseverance the race marked out for us, fixing our eyes on Jesus, the pioneer and perfecter of faith. For the joy set before him he endured the Cross, scorning its shame, and sat down at the right hand of the throne of God."*

When we fix our eyes on Jesus, our hearts are postured toward Him, operating in obedience to Him. Sin loses its grip, because our focus isn't on sin, but is rightly fixed on the author of our faith. He took on the Cross so that we may surrender our lives to Him, daily dying to ourselves, thereby throwing off sin that easily entangles. We cannot see the Bible as a set of laws to memorize and white-knuckle. We must address the heart condition.

Heart Condition

Jeremiah 17:9 says:

> *"The heart is deceitful above all things and beyond cure. Who can understand it?"*

When we scrutinize and examine our behavior without looking at the heart, we are not looking to fix the problem, but rather to modify what can be seen on the outside. It's like a nasty weed that is "treated" by pulling off the top part of the plant. If the top part of the weed is the only part that is removed, it will grow back. The real problem exists much deeper that what is on the surface. The problem lies deep down in the dirt, in the roots. The same is the case with us: our biggest problem lies deep in our hearts. The external behavior on the outside is the reflection of what lies on the inside, with our hearts. We must understand this to properly pin point where sin comes from, so we know where to ask the Holy Spirit to do work. The desires of our hearts must be transformed and will be transformed as we walk with Christ daily. When the desires of our heart change, our plans will also change along with them.

David captures this paradigm in Psalm 37:4:

> *"Take delight in the Lord, and he will give you the desires of your heart."*

"What the heart loves, the will chooses, and the mind justifies."
--Theologian Thomas Crammer

Understand that the mind doesn't direct the will; the mind and the will are both subject to and at the mercy of the heart. Therefore, let our hearts be right before God, fixed upon Jesus in life-long obedience and worship, service and glorification. Out of this posture will the rhythms of our life be as they are intended, uninterrupted by the dysfunction and dualism of sin. The bottom line is when a person comes to faith in Christ, he must choose to believe that, due to Jesus' death on the Cross, every Christian must die to sin and focus daily on resisting temptation.

Ron Proctor

Offer Your Body as an Instrument of Righteousness Every Day

It is important for you to understand that the righteousness we have as believers is not our own but belongs to Jesus. It is given to all who might believe in Him (John 3:16) and was provided for on the Cross when Jesus took on our sin (2 Corinthians 5:21). **One of the biggest temptations you will face on a daily basis is to validate yourself to God and to man.** That daily tendency to take more pride in our victories than we ought, that need we have to point to our goodness as if it will make God loves us more. Thankfully, that is not how it works! Jesus did not die for a future "better" version of us, but rather paid for us while we were still sinners (Romans 5:8). The love of God is not contingent on our performance or the righteousness we think we muster up for ourselves. It is unconditional, meaning that it surpasses all things and is unhindered by our failures. The Bible says that we were chosen before the foundation of the world to be blameless before Him (Ephesians 1:4). Therefore, offering our bodies as instruments of righteousness is a deliberate and honest day-to-day surrender of our lives back to him.

Understand this again: our righteousness is not our own! This is simultaneously the most liberating and motivating reality we can ever understand. **Properly understanding where our righteousness comes from keeps us from becoming self-righteous, which means doing religious things for how it makes us look rather than operating in obedience to and worship of our Savior.** How we understand the source of our righteousness will determine whether we go through life living like a pious Pharisee or a humble disciple of Jesus. We will explore both sides of this contrast in this lesson, as we understand the importance of daily sacrifice to Jesus continually looking to Him as our model.

Link together these two ways of living: Die to sin every day and live a righteous life.

There was only one who lived a righteous life and His name was Jesus. Therefore, the key to living a righteous life is to let Jesus live His life in and through us every day. So how do we live that way continuously? It isn't easy to understand that we are no longer living for ourselves, but the Bible tells us how that is possible.

Romans 6:12-13 says:

"Do not let sin reign in your mortal body, so that you obey its evil desires. Do not offer any part of yourself to sin as an instrument of wickedness but rather offer yourselves to God as those who have been brought from death to life; and offer every part of yourself to Him as an instrument of righteousness."

Looking to Jesus as our model, we must daily sacrifice our bodies as instruments of righteousness every day. Living a righteous life can only be accomplished by realizing daily that we have already died to ourselves and to sin. When we humbly see the righteousness we have as God-given, we are more likely to give God the glory He deserves than make much of ourselves.

Why is it so important to offer our bodies to righteousness every day? Galatians 5:16-24 tells us that when we yield to our flesh or sin, our flesh is in constant conflict with the Spirit of God. The key to producing the characteristics of the Holy Spirit of God is to offer my body to God as an instrument of righteousness every day. When I do this, I will be living by the Spirit, not by the flesh, mindful of what I am able to overcome by the power of the Spirit. Christians must live by the Spirit in order to put to death sins like sexual immorality, impurity, jealousy, hatred, fits of rage, drunkenness, and selfish ambitions.

As a believer, living by the flesh is no longer something I have the right to exercise. The Bible speaks of me as a new creation, with old desires taken off and new desires put on (2 Corinthi-ans 5:17), living each day by the Spirit. When I walk each day by the Spirit, I no longer gratify what my flesh wants me to take part in. I understand that this is a daily struggle in which I must consistently depend on the Spirit's help to convict me of sin and empower me to no longer walk in sin.

Romans 6:6-7 says:

> *"For we know that our old self was crucified with him so that the body ruled by sin might be done away with, that we should no longer be slaves to sin—because anyone who has died has been set free from sin."*

When I gave my heart to Jesus Christ, I gave up the right to live my life the way I wanted to. If I still try to control my life, I cannot properly let Him reign as the sovereign Lord of my life.

Romans 6:11-13 says:

> *"In the same way, count yourselves dead to sin but alive to God in Christ Jesus. Therefore do not let sin reign in your mortal body, so that you obey its evil desires. Do not off any part of yourself to sin as an instrument*

of wickedness but rather offer yourselves to God as those who have been brought from death to life; and offer every part of yourself to Him as an instrument of righteousness."

When I received Christ, I died to myself and sin is not supposed to dominate me. That means I gave up the right to live my life the way I choose, and my new goal is to yield myself to God every day. I must remember to place the outcome of my life in the all-knowing and all-powerful hands of God who gave His Son for me.
Colossians 3:1-3 says:

"Since, then, you have been raised with Christ, set your hearts on things above, where Christ is, seated at the right hand of God. Set your minds on things above, not on earthly things. For you died, and your life is now hidden with Christ in God."

This verse teaches us these important principles to live by:

1. Live each day remembering that you died.

2. Your life is now hidden with Christ in God.

3. Your life no longer belongs to you but is hidden with Christ.

4. Set aside those earthly things that you medicate your brokenness with.

5. Set the ultimate desire of your heart on things above.

Ron Proctor

Two Steps to Living in Righteousness

If you desire to offer yourself as an instrument of righteousness, practice the following steps each day for a whole week. Ask the Holy Spirit for help as you look to make these steps a routine: steeped in worshipful obedience to God who is Holy, postured in selfless surrender to our Savior who gave His life for us.

Step 1: Realize that if I live my Christian life in my own power I will fail to honor God with my life.

1 Corinthians 2:14 says:

> *"The person without the Spirit does not accept the things that come from the Spirit of God but considers them foolishness, and cannot understand them because they are discerned only through the Spirit."*

Jeremiah 17:9 says:

> *"The heart is deceitful above all things and beyond cure. Who can under-stand it?"*

Romans 3:10-17 says:

> *"There is no one righteous, not even one; there is no one who understand; there is no one who seeks God. All have turned away, they have together become worthless; there is no one who does good, not even one. Their throats are open*

graves; their tongues practice deceit. The poison of vipers is on their lips. Their mouths are full of cursing and bitterness. Their feet are swift to shed blood; ruin and misery mark their ways, and the way of peace they do not know."

When we try and live a God honoring life in our own power, we will look within ourselves to make it happen. We will try and succeed in our own strength, which is puny compared to an Almighty God, based on our perception of things, which is extremely limited compared to an Omniscient God. When we do not look to His strength, we will continue to struggle with the idols in our lives.

At times we fail to depend on His Holy Spirit because living a life that honors God would mean we have to give up certain **things**. Think about your own life. Do you tend to look to material things to define you rather than looking to your identity in Christ? When we look to these things, they become our idols that we seemingly cannot destroy because of their importance to us. We have let them take on more significance than they were ever intended to have because we have given into the lie that they give us meaning and worth.

We must understand that they will only sustain us for so long before someone else has more than we do or is better than we are. We must see that this process of defining who we are, based on what we have, keeps us from presenting ourselves to God. We know that the items themselves are not the problem, rather it's the condition of the heart where the real problem lies.

Ultimately, this process reflects that we haven't let the significance and sacrifice of the Cross of Jesus Christ communicate to us how much we mean to God.

When we fail to see that, we will look to other means to prove ourselves worthy, at the expense of the Cross. In our culture, we thrive on acceptance and approval. Even if it means we turn our back on the Cross, we will do anything to get it. Do not let yourself become enslaved to the idol of acceptance, confined to the chains of culture and success. Liberation is found in the daily sacrifice of our lives, which are no longer ours and are hidden with Christ (Colossians 3:3), to God through the power of His Holy Spirit. Only then can we honor God with our whole life.

Step 2: Realize your responsibility to live supernaturally every day.

Galatians 5:16-24 teaches us how to live this kind of life.

1. If I live my life under the control of the Holy Spirit, I will not gratify the sinful nature.
2. My flesh and the Holy Spirit are battling inside my life to encourage me to sin or to produce the Fruit of the Holy Spirit.
3. The acts of the sinful nature dishonor God.
4. The Fruit of the Holy Spirit is to honor God.
5. The key is to walk under the control of the Holy Spirit every day.
6. I must not look to my own strength for a God honoring life.

7. I must understand my own tendency to point to my own self-righteousness thereby denying the work of God in me.

We have covered in depth the struggles we face each day with living the God honoring life. Hopefully, this chapter has made you aware of the tendencies in human nature to walk in the flesh rather than the Spirit. By God's grace, you may have been able to see your own inclination to look to insignificant things to try and find significance.

Remember:
The Cross is a reminder that God has done wonderful things for us!

The reason we do that is for recognition and pronouncement of our own glory. When we operate in this way, we are using the breath that God grants us and the bodies God has given us to rob Him of the glory that is due to Him. It's what Martin Luther called "theologians of glory," acting out of our own best interests rather than giving glory through our actions to the God who is to be forever praised. Sadly, we can spend many of our days in this life fishing horizontally for what has been provided vertically. We must strive to become Christians that are continually mindful of the righteousness granted at the Cross and respond to the Cross with our lifelong offerings as instruments of reflection back to the Cross.

Know This:
One who rightly understands the Cross will be found under the Cross pointing others to the Cross.

CHAPTER THREE

EMPTYING YOUR EMOTIONAL CUP

Emotional pain is unavoidable. Forty years ago, I finished seminary. Then, I went to work for a church full time, where I stayed for six weeks before they fired me. That termination was devastating because I thought all my self-worth was tied to what I do. I soon discovered that my self-worth is actually tied to my identity in Christ. I still do not know why I was fired, but I learned how to deal with the pain by emptying my emotional cup.

This lesson is about getting rid of anything that gets in the way of your identity in Christ.

Life is full of painful experiences. In order to live a full life and maintain healthy relationships, we must deal with the hurt, disappointment, and sadness that comes as a result of those experiences.

We can work to sidestep it by acquiring money, success, and friendships or try to drown it in alcohol and work, but there are just distractions from the inevitable. All our attempts at denying the hurt we have encountered only reduce our potential for living out a victorious life Christ promised us.

Fortunately, there is a way to deal with the hurt, disappointment, and sadness that we encounter so that we can find comfort. Then we can live our lives full of joy and purpose, having healthy relationships with those people God has placed in our influence.

Ron Proctor

Always remember that unresolved pain produces a full cup.

As they were moving into their new home, they met their next-door neighbor, Martha. As they were just moving in, Martha came over. Without an introduction, she made it clear that she did not like children or dogs and did not want them anywhere near her property.

Jason and Lynne were dismayed at Martha's attitude, but they decided that the godliest way to handle the situation would be to be patient with her and show her love. Once, when Jason was mowing his yard, he decided to mow Martha's as well. When Martha came home and discovered what he had done, she yelled at Jason. She threatened to press changes for trespassing if he ever did it again.

One Sunday afternoon, Lynne left some muffins at Martha's door with a note of encouragement. However, the next morning, the entire basket of muffins was at Jason and Lynne's door. Martha had written her own note, which said that she neither appreciated nor wanted their muffins, and they should keep them to themselves.

After a few years, Jason decided to move for work to another town. They felt discouraged that they never had a good relationship with Martha. At times they blamed themselves for not being better Christians. Yet they did not know what else they could have done to reach out to such a malicious person.

As they were loading boxes onto the moving van, Martha approached Jason and said, "You do not know anything about me, do you?"

"No, Martha, I don't," Jason answered.

"My daughter, my only child, is in a nursing home."

Martha replied. "I put her there thirty years ago because I could not care for her anymore. Do you know why I could not care for her?"

"Why is that?" Jason asked.

Forgiveness Fact or Fiction? - Volume 2 - IDENTITY

"She is an invalid. When she was a toddler, I did not see her in the driveway as I came home from work. I hit her with the car. She almost died. I did that to my own daughter. I do not deserve for anyone to do kind things for me. I do not deserve your kindness, and I do not deserve to be **forgiven**."

What Jason and Lynne and the rest of us can learn from Martha's story is that we do not know what other people are experiencing. We do not know what has happened in their lives to make them feel and act the way they do.

The pain we experience in life manifests itself in ways that may not seem to have anything to do with what has happened to cause us to feel that pain. Anyone who has experienced a devastating loss can respond to the pain of their loss in completely different ways, but one thing they all need is to be comforted in their hurt. Comfort helps us heal. When we walk through life with unaddressed pain, **we tend to inflict pain on those around us**. You may think you're managing your emotional pain, but you're really just camouflaging it with toxic emotions and negative behaviors.

How many times have you been hurt by a friend's careless comment but did not deal with the sadness you felt because you convinced yourself it was not a big deal? The problem with this approach is that when you allow enough negative emotions to build up within you (full emotional cup), you expend much of your emotional energy just trying to hold In feelings that are poisoning you.

Ron Proctor

Any hurt, disappointment, and sadness you felt is a result of a painful experience. So, the best way to deal with your hurt, disappointment, and sadness is to deal with your pain.

Imagine that we all carry with us and inner cup specifically to hold our emotion. This emotional cup has a limited capacity and will overflow if the hurt and pain we put in it is not dealt with and emptied. We can only push down emotions for so long. When the cup finally overflows with all our negative, emotions, it results in negative displays of behavior, which in turn interfere with our relationship—both with God and the people we love the most.

When you look at the image of an emotional cup filled with painful emotions, you may wonder how a person with so much hurt, disappointment, and sadness in his or her life can get out of the cycle of taking in the pain until it overflows and causes more destruction.

Forgiveness Fact or Fiction? - Volume 2 - IDENTITY

Fortunately, when the temptation to react to a person or situation with hurt, disappointment and sadness arises, God, Himself wants to meet us in our pain so that our emotional cups can produce a heart that chooses to **forgive**, **bless**, and **rejoice**. Remember your own forgiveness. The key to doing that is visiting the Cross every day. Remember what Jesus has done for you.

> "When they hurled their insults at him, he did not retaliate; when he suffered, he made no threats. Instead, he entrusted himself to him, who judges justly. 24 "He Himself bore our sins" in his body on the cross, so that we might die to sins and live for righteousness; "by his wounds, you have been healed."
>
> 1 Peter 2: 23-24

Ron Proctor

How do you not respond when you experience hurt?

How do you not respond when you get disappointed?

How do you not respond when you receive sadness from others?

- We are supposed to **forgive**

    "Be kind and compassionate to one another, forgiving each other, just as in Christ God forgave you."
    Ephesians 4:32

- We are supposed to **bless**

    "Finally, all of you, be like-minded, be sympathetic, love one another, be compassionate and humble. 9 Do not repay evil with evil or insult with insult. On the contrary, repay evil with blessing, because to this you were called so that you may inherit a blessing."
    1 Peter 3:8-9

- We are supposed to **throw a party**

   "James, a servant of God and of the Lord Jesus Christ, to the twelve tribes scattered among the nations: Greetings. Consider it pure joy, my brothers and sisters, whenever you face trials of many kinds."
   James 1:1-2

How do we do that amid hurt, pain, and disappointment?

There are five steps.

1. Realize God's word is true and perfect.

   "As for God, his way is perfect: The Lord's word is flawless; he shields all who take refuge in him."
   Psalm 18:30

   "The law of the Lord is perfect, refreshing the soul. The statutes of the Lord are trustworthy, making wise the simple."
   Psalm 19:7

   "All your words are true; all your righteous laws are eternal."
   Psalm 119:160

2. Realize God has called us to live by Faith.

> *"And without faith it is impossible to please God because anyone who comes to him must believe that he exists and that he rewards those who earnestly seek him."*
> Hebrews 11:6

> *"But whoever has doubts is condemned if they eat, because their eating is not from faith; and everything that does not come from faith is sin."*
> Romans 14:23

> *"For we live by faith, not by sight."*
> 2 Corinthians 5:7

3. Realize God wants to conform you to the image of his son.

> *"In the same way, the Spirit helps us in our weakness. We do not know what we ought to pray for, but the Spirit Himself intercedes for us through wordless groans. And He who searches our hearts knows the mind of the Spirit because the Spirit intercedes for God's people in accordance with the will of God. And we know that in all things God works for the good of those who love Him, who have been called according to His purpose. For those God foreknew He also predestined to be conformed to the image of his Son, that He might be the firstborn among many brothers and sisters. And those He predestined, He also called; those He called, He also justified; those He justified, He also glorified."*
> Romans 8:26

4. Realize that the spirit of God wants to comfort your heart. Only then you will be able to *forgive, bless* and *rejoice*.

"Praise be to the God and Father of our Lord Jesus Christ, the Father of compassion and the God of all comfort, who comforts us in all our troubles so that we can comfort those in any trouble with the comfort we ourselves receive from God."
2 Corinthians 1:3-4

5. Realize that God will ALWAYS love you.

"For God so loved the world that he gave his one and only Son, that whoever believes in him shall not perish but have eternal life."
John 3:16

Dealing with Negative Emotions

God wants us to deal with our negative emotions. If negative emotions are not properly dealt with, most people will default to one of these:

Self-Indulgence: Sometimes, we are selfish, and we do whatever it takes to heal our pain. Philippians 2:3 says, "Do nothing out of selfish ambition or vain conceit. Rather, in humility, value others above yourselves."

Self- Reliance: Sometimes, we depend on ourselves to deal with our pain. Revelation 3:17 says, "You say, 'I am rich; I have acquired wealth and do not need a thing.' But you do not realize that you are wretched, pitiful, poor, blind, and naked."

Self-Condemnation: Sometimes, we blame ourselves for our pain, and we end up feeling guilty, condemned, and ashamed. Romans 8:1 says, "Therefore, there is now no condemnation for those who are in Christ Jesus."

Understanding Relational Needs

God has designed us to have relational needs. When we experience relational emotions, He wants to meet us there in our pain. One of the things that could be helpful is to know why certain things are so painful, and to understand how God has wired us relationally.

God has made us to connect with Him and with others.

We need Him, and we need others. In Genesis 2:18, He says, "It is not good for the man to be alone." 1 Corinthians 12:12-27, the Apostle Paul used the example of the human body to illustrate how Christians are dependent upon each other. To experience the intimacy that God intends in our relationship, we must understand that Christ wants us to be godly comfort to those people He has placed in our lives, and He wants us to experience that comfort from Him as well.

The hurt in our lives highlights our emotional needs, but we are not all the same. Someone who needs affection may try to comfort a person in pain by showing her affection. If that person's biggest emotional need is support, however, she will not feel comforted. That is why it is important to know what those needs are.

An important aspect of loving others is knowing where their properties lie regarding their relational needs. One person may need affection while another may need respect, and still another person may need acceptance. If you have a better understanding of what an individual needs from you, your attempts to relate to them will be more productive and personal. You may also want to look carefully at those needs to discover what your relational needs are.

We have looked at the emotional pain that we have in our lives. We have looked at how God wants to respond to us in our pain and how He wants us to respond to Him and others. We have looked at self-centered ways to respond to negative emotion and how God wired us relationally and emotionally.

Matthew 26:36-46 tells about Jesus time in the garden and His deep hurt, disappointment, and sadness. He said to His disciples that His soul was deeply grieved to the point of death, hurt beyond our understanding. He asked His disappointment when He came back three times and found them all asleep? Considering that, we can see how Jesus can relate to our hurt, disappointment, and sadness in our pain. Remember the Faith definition always.

<u>Faith Definition:</u>
Faith is choosing to live as though the Bible
is true regardless of circumstances, emotions
or cultural trends.

It may be difficult for you to claim the faith process at times. Remember, God's Word is true, regardless of how we feel. Sometimes the hurt we experience leads to unresolved anger.

Ron Proctor

> "Be kind and compassionate to one another, **forgiving** each other, just as in Christ God forgave you."
> Ephesians 4:32

> "James, a servant of God and of the Lord Jesus Christ, To the twelve tribes scattered among the nations: Greetings. **Consider it pure joy**, my brothers and sisters, whenever you face trials of many kinds."
> James 1:1-2

> "To sum up, all of you be harmonious, sympathetic, brotherly, kindhearted, and humble in spirit; not returning evil for evil or insult for insult but giving a **blessing** instead; for you were called for the very purpose that you might inherit a blessing."
> 1 Peter 3:8-9

If we are living as though the Bible is true and disregarding circumstances, emotions, or cultural trends, then we must forgive and with unresolved anger.

Sometimes we just don't feel like blessing someone! But if we choose to walk in faith, we choose to bless instead of return evil or insult.

When you find yourself on the receiving end of someone else's hurtful words or actions, the best reaction is not one of anger or retaliation but to stop and say a prayer asking God to:

1. Comfort my pain.

2. Help me forgive the person who has hurt me.

3. Give me the strength to bless the person who has injured me.

If the hurt is unresolved, there could be a temptation to respond to people with negative emotions and behaviors. Once you have experienced the comfort of God's love, He wants you to be His ambassador by loving others the way He loves you—unconditionally.

I encourage you to take this test, discover your relational needs, and act appropriately.

Ron Proctor

Relational Need Questionnaire

While we all have the same realtional needs, the *priority* of those needs is different for each person. Your greatest need may be for *afftection*, while your partner's greatest need may be *security*; but another sibling's greatest need may be encouragement. *Appreciation* may be at the top of the list for your nextdoor neighbor, while your tennis buddy need *approval* more than anything else.

An important aspect of learning to love others is taking the time to know them and to discover what their priority needs are. This questionnaire will help you assess your most important relational needs.Take the time to carefully and thoughtfully answer the following questions, then score the questionnaire to identify which needs you perceived as most important. have family members, friends, and ministry team members complete the quesitonnaire and then discuss the results.

Instructions: Respond to these questions by placing the appropriate number beside each item, using this scale:

Strongly Disagree	Disagree	Neutral	Agree	Strongly Agree
-2	-1	0	+1	+2

_____ 1. It is important that people receive me for who I am, even if I am a little different.

_____ 2. It is important to me that my financial world is in order.

_____ 3. I sometimes become "weary in well-doing."

_____ 4. It is vital to me that others ask my opinion.

_____ 5. It is important to me that I receive physical hugs, warm embraces, etc.

_____ 6. I feel good when someone "enters into my world."

Forgiveness Fact or Fiction? - Volume 2 - IDENTITY

_____ 7. It is important for me to "know where I stand" with those who are in authority over me.

_____ 8. It is meaningful when someone notices that I need help and they offer to get involved.

_____ 9. If I feel overwhelmed, I want someone to come alongside me and help.

_____ 10. I feel blessed when someone recognizes and shows concern for how I am feeling.

_____ 11. I like to know if "who I am" is of value and is meaningful to others.

_____ 12. It is important to me to express myself (what I think, feel, etc.) to those around me.

_____ 13. It means a lot to me for loved ones to initiate saying to me, "I love you."

_____ 14. I resist being seen as a part of a large group. My individuality is important.

_____ 15. I am blessed when a friend calls to listen and encourage me.

_____ 16. It is important to me that people acknowledge me not just for what I do but also for who I am.

_____ 17. I feel best when my world is orderly and somewhat predictable.

_____ 18. When I have worked hard on something, I am pleased when others express gratitude.

_____ 19. When I "blow it," it is important to me to be reassured that I am still loved.

_____ 20. It is encouraging to me that others notice my effort or accomplishments.

Ron Proctor

_____ 21. I sometimes feel overwhelmed with all I have to do.

_____ 22. I want to be treated with kindness and equality by all regardless of my race, gender, looks, or status.

_____ 23. I like to be greeted with a handshake or other appropriate friendly touch.

_____ 24. I like it when someone wants to spend time with me.

_____ 25. I am blessed when a "superior" says, "Good job."

_____ 26. It is important to me for someone to express care for me after I have had a hard day.

_____ 27. When facing something difficult, I usually sense that I need other people's input and help.

_____ 28. Written notes and calls expressing sympathy after a serious loss or difficulty are (or would be) meaningful to me.

_____ 29. I feel good when someone close to me shows satisfaction with the way I am.

_____ 30. I enjoy being spoken of or mentioned in front of other people.

_____ 31. I would be described as someone who likes hugs and/or other caring touches.

_____ 32. When a decision is going to affect me, it is important that I am involved in the decision.

_____ 33. I am blessed when someone shows interest in what I am working on.

_____ 34. I appreciate trophies, plaques or special gifts as permanent reminders of something significant I have done.

_____ 35. I sometimes worry about the future.

Forgiveness Fact or Fiction? - Volume 2 - IDENTITY

_____ 36. When I am introduced into a new environment, I typically search for a group to connect with.

_____ 37. The thought of changing (moving, new job, etc.) produces anxiety for me.

_____ 38. It bothers me when people are prejudiced against someone just because they dress or act differently.

_____ 39. I want to be close friends with loved ones who will be there through "thick and thin."

_____ 40. I am blessed by written notes and other specific expressions of gratitude.

_____ 41. To know that someone is praying for me is meaningful to me.

_____ 42. I am bothered by "controlling" people.

_____ 43. I am blessed when I receive unmerited and spontaneous expressions of love.

_____ 44. I am pleased when someone carefully listens to me.

_____ 45. I am blessed when people commend me for a godly characteristic I exhibit.

_____ 46. I typically do not want to be alone when experiencing hurt and trouble.

_____ 47. I do not enjoy working on a project by myself. I prefer to have a partner.

_____ 48. It is important to me to feel as a "part of the group."

_____ 49. I respond to someone who tries to understand me and who shows me loving concern.

_____ 50. I would rather work with a team of people than by myself.

Now add up your responses (-2, -1, 0, +1, +2) according to the following criteria:

1. Add up your responses to items:
   - 1 _____
   - 19 _____
   - 36 _____
   - 38 _____
   - 48 _____

Total _____

These responses relate to the need for **ACCEPTANCE**.

2. Add up your responses to items:
   - 5 _____
   - 13 _____
   - 23 _____
   - 31 _____
   - 43 _____

Total _____

These responses relate to the need for **AFFECTION**.

3. Add up your responses to items:
    - 18 _____
    - 20 _____
    - 25 _____
    - 34 _____
    - 40 _____

Total _____

These responses relate to the need for **APPRECIATION**.

4. Add up your responses to items:
    - 7 _____
    - 11 _____
    - 16 _____
    - 29 _____
    - 45 _____

Total _____

These responses relate to the need for **APPROVAL**.

5. Add up your responses to items:
    - 6 _____
    - 12 _____
    - 24 _____
    - 30 _____
    - 44 _____

Total _____

These responses relate to the need for **ATTENTION**.

Ron Proctor

6. Add up your responses to items:
   - 10 _____
   - 26 _____
   - 28 _____
   - 46 _____
   - 49 _____

Total _____

These responses relate to the need for **COMFORT**.

7. Add up your responses to items:
   - 3 _____
   - 15 _____
   - 21 _____
   - 33 _____
   - 41 _____

Total _____

These responses relate to the need for **ENCOURAGEMENT**.

8. Add up your responses to items:
   - 4 _____
   - 14 _____
   - 22 _____
   - 32 _____
   - 42 _____

Total _____

These responses relate to the need for **RESPECT**.

9. Add up your responses to items:
   - 2 _____
   - 17 _____
   - 35 _____
   - 37 _____
   - 39 _____

Total _____

These responses relate to the need for **SECURITY**.

10. Add up your responses to items:
    - 8 _____
    - 9 _____
    - 27 _____
    - 47 _____
    - 50 _____

Total _____

These responses relate to the need for **SUPPORT**.

DISCUSS

What three needs scored the highest? Why do you think these needs scored as high as they did?

Ron Proctor

What three needs scored the lowest? Why do you think these needs scored as low as they did?

Our Relational Needs

ACCEPTANCE: to receive another person willingly and unconditionally when the other's behavior has been imperfect and to be willing to continue to love that person in spite of his or her offenses.

> "Accept one another, then, just as Christ accepted you, in order to bring praise to God."
> Romans 15:7

AFFECTION: to express kindness and caring through physical touch or speech.

> "And he took the children in his arms, placed his hands on them, and blessed them."
> Mark 10:16

> "Greet one another with a holy kiss."
> Romans 16:16a

Forgiveness Fact or Fiction? - Volume 2 - IDENTITY

APPRECIATION: To express thanks, praise, or commendation; to recognize accomplishment or effort.

> *"I praise you for remembering me in everything and for holding to the traditions just as I passed them on to you."*
> 1 Corinthians 11:2

> *"... And be thankful."*
> Colossians 3:15b

APPROVAL: To build up or affirm another.

> *"And a voice came from heaven: You are my Son, whom I love; with you I am well pleased."*
> Mark 1:11

> *"Do not let any unwholesome talk come out of your mouths, but only what is helpful for building others up according to their needs, that it may benefit those who listen."*
> Ephesians 4:29

ATTENTION: To convey appropriate interest, concern, and care to take thought of another and enter his or her world.

> *"So that there should be no division in the body, but that its parts should have equal concern for each other."*
> 1 Corinthians 12:25

COMFORT: to respond to a hurting person with words, feelings, and touch; to hurt with and for another's grief or pain.

> "Blessed are those who mourn,
> for they will be comforted."
> Matthew 5:4

> "Jesus wept."
> John 11:35

> "... Mourn with those who mourn."
> Romans 12:5b

> "Grace and peace to you from God our Father and the Lord Jesus Christ. I always thank my God for you because of his grace given you in Christ Jesus."
> 1 Corinthians 1:3-4

ENCOURAGEMENT: To urge another to persist, persevere toward a goal.

> "And let us consider how we may spur one another on toward love and good deeds"
> Hebrews 10:24

> "Therefore encourage one another and build each other up, just as in fact you are doing."
> 1 Thessalonians 5:11

RESPECT: To value and regard another person highly, to honor and treat another person as important.

> *"Be devoted to one another in love. Honor one another above yourselves."*
> Romans 12:10

SECURITY (peace): To have harmony in relationships, to have freedom from fear or threat of harm.

> *"Be of the same mind toward one another; do not be haughty in mind, but [a]associate with the lowly. Do not be wise in your own estimation. If possible, so far as it depends on you, be at peace with all men."*
> Romans 12:16,18

SUPPORT: To come alongside and gently help another person with a problem or struggle, to provide appropriate assistance.

> *"Carry each other's burdens, and in this way, you will fulfill the law of Christ."*
> Galatians 6:2

CHAPTER FOUR

APPLYING THE FAITH PROCESS

Making it REAL

In this chapter, we are going to explore what it means to live according to your identity in Christ. We will take a look at ten verses and see what it means to live by faith according to what these verses say. We will do so by taking each verse through the FAITH PROCESS.

> **Faith Definition:**
> Faith is choosing to live as though the Bible is true, regardless of circumstances, emotions or cultural trends.

1. Review the Faith Definition.

2. Ask yourself; "If I were living as though this passage of Scripture were true, then how would I be living?" Use this question to help you apply every Scripture you read.

3. Pray for the Holy Spirit's help. You cannot do this alone. At salvation, God gave you the Holy Spirit to guide you. Ask Him for His help in living out what you learn in Scripture.

Ron Proctor

LET'S LOOK AT TEN VERSES TO SEE HOW GOD'S WORD CAN BECOME REAL IN YOU LIFE WITH THE HELP OF THE HOLY SPIRIT

SUGGESTION:

- Take the next ten days reading one verse a day.

- Read and think about what the verse means to you. Pray asking God for wisdom.

- Read the information on the page and use a journal to write down your notes.

- End by praying the prayer given or your own prayer of commitment to living out the verse for the day.

DAY ONE:

"FAITH makes obstacles into helps, and stones of stumbling into 'stepping stones to Higher things."
Matthew Henry

DAY ONE

"I have been crucified with Christ and I no longer live, but Christ lives in me. The life I now live in the body, I live by faith in the Son of God, who loved me and gave himself for me."

Galatians 2:20

As you think of the first sentence in that verse, imagine your life like this:

As you look at the Cross above think of it this way: *"I no longer live, but Christ lives in me."* The old person is gone. My heart no longer lives. My old self died on the Cross when I gave my life to Jesus. My old desires have been crucified with Christ. Now the new person lives. That new creation is Christ living in me.

Can I do this alone? No. But the life I now live I live by walking in faith every day. Faith in who? In what? I must walk in faith in the person who loved me so much that he gave Himself for me.

If I were living according to Galatians 2:20, how would I be living.

- I would know that my will and my old, sinful heart have been crucified.

- I am a new person.

- I live each day by faith. I don't know what is going to happen, but I can trust the One who does.

- Jesus loved me and gave Himself for me.

- My faith is in Jesus. I cannot put my faith in friends, money, leaders.

- Treat other Christians knowing that Christ lives in them also and help them in their venture to live this out.

As Christians we have the God's Holy Spirit to walk with us, to teach us and to convict us. We have to ask the Holy Spirit to help us live each day according to Galatians 2:20.

Consider this prayer:

Holy Spirit, I need you. I know I am a new person in Christ. I want to live each day by faith in the One who loved me enough to die for me. Help me to put my faith in you instead of in things of the world and my own flesh. Amen

DAY TWO

"God made him who had no sin to be sin for us, so that in him we might become the righteousness of God."

2 Corinthians 5:21

Forgiveness Fact or Fiction? - Volume 2 - **IDENTITY**

Picture this:

On the Cross, Jesus took on all our sin. He paid the ultimate price to make a way for us to live a life free from the debt of sin. Yes, we sin. But we do not have to live feeling guilty. What we can know is that the guilt of our sin was placed on Jesus' back as He hung on the Cross. Today we can walk in His righteousness, not our own.

If I live as if 2 Corinthians 5:21 is true, how would I be living?

- I would remember that Christ died for me and thank Him.

- I would understand that God has also forgiven other Christians and I would forgive them as well.

- Know that I can walk in righteousness.

- Know that other Christians are walking the same path.

- My Christian relationships need to be a healthy reflection of walking together in righteousness.

Consider this prayer:

God, I cannot do this alone. Without you, I cannot walk in righteousness. I am so thankful for Christ's death on the Cross. I will never comprehend the debt of His love for me. Help me to live each day in gratitude for that love and sacrifice. Help me to walk in righteousness with all Christians.

DAY THREE

"Therefore do not let sin reign in your mortal body so that you obey its evil desires, Do not offer any part of yourself to sin as an instrument of wickedness; but rather offer yourselves to God as those who have been bought from death to life: and offer every part of yourself to him as an instrument of righteousness."

Romans 6:12-13

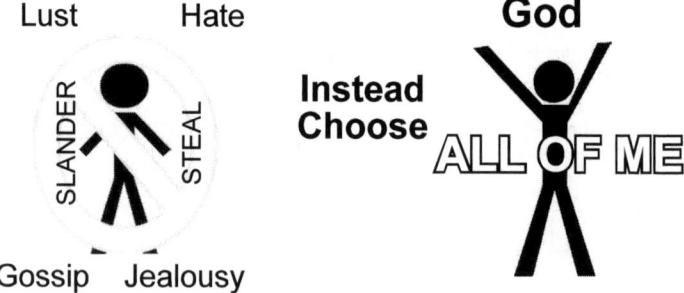

Where do you see yourself?

As believers, we cannot let sin be the driving factor in our lives. If we choose that path, we will live a defeated Christian life and that is exactly what Satan would like to see. The Christian life can be so much more. If we offer ourselves to God, every part of ourselves, we will live in His righteousness. We will honor Him with our lives!

If I am living according to Romans 6:12-13, how would I be living?

- Sin would not take over my body.

- Therefore, I would not give into fleshly desires or wickedness.

- Instead, my whole life is offered to Him, for the choices He has for me.

- As I deal with other Christians, I will not choose to use slander or jealousy or hatred or gossip; any of the choices the devil tries to pull me into.

- I will help other Christians along this path of making right choices by being the example.

Consider this prayer:

Holy Spirit, convict me of my sin. (Confess any sins and ask forgiveness.) Help me to put these sins behind me. I want to give all of myself to you. I do not want to hold back any part of myself. As I deal with my brothers and sisters in Christ, help me not to be a stumbling block. Help them to see you in me. And help me to see you in them. Amen.

DAY FOUR

"Therefore, there is now no condemnation for those who are in Christ Jesus."
Romans 8:1

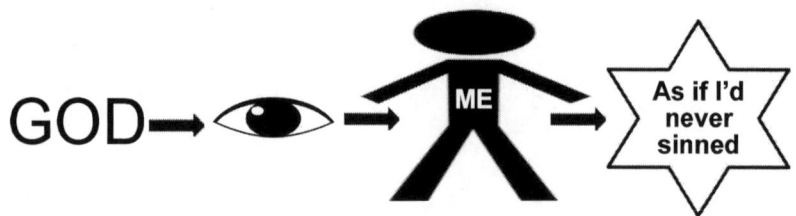

How does it make you feel to know that God sees you as if you'd never sinned? Romans 8:1 tells us that God sees us that way. When we accept Christ, we move out from under the umbrella of the condemned under the umbrella of Christ Jesus. God no longer sees me as a condemned sinner but as a redeemed child of His.

If I were living according to Romans 8:1, how would I be living?

- I understand that God no longer sees me as condemned.

- Accepting Jesus is my hope for freedom from condemnation.

- I now live IN Christ Jesus and He lives IN me.

- This verse applies to all Christians; therefore, I must treat them as Jesus would.

- If Jesus does not condemn my Christian acquaintances, then I should not either.

Consider this prayer:

"Dear Jesus, thank you for taking on my condemnation on the Cross. I need help to understand this concept because many times

I condemn myself. I want to live in the freedom you offer. Thank you for moving into my dirty, rotten old self and cleaning it up to make it pure like you. Help me as I deal with my emotions toward others. Help me be the example I need to be in forgiveness, not condemning. Amen."

DAY FIVE

"Therefore, if anyone is in Christ, the new creation has come: The old has gone, the new is here."
2 Corinthians 5:17

    Consider the change that is made from the caterpillar to the butterfly. The caterpillar is the old creature. Through the total transformation in the cocoon, it emerges as the new creation of a butterfly. A change takes place. Nothing is the same. The old creature is gone and the new is here.
    That is a perfect picture of 2 Corinthians 5:17. When a person totally submits to God by accepting Christ as Savior, a change takes place. All the old is gone and the new person comes forth. Jesus erases the past of sin and gives us a new life of righteousness. That is not an easy transformation because the new life requires death to old ways, ego, and sometimes letting go of past friendships.

But the new life that Christ has for the believer is so much better and beautiful, like the life of the butterfly.

If I am living as though 2 Corinthians 5:17 is true, how will I be living?

- I will submit to Christ totally, allowing Him to make changes in my life.

- I begin to recognize the newness of what He offers me.

- When things from my past creep back into my life, I put them behind again and confess any sin.

- I walk daily depending on the Holy Spirit to keep me living in the new way of life.

- I treat other Christians as if they are also new creations.

- My attitude toward fellow believers must be to walk alongside them to help them and allow them to help me.

Consider this prayer:

"Father, I know I am no longer the same. Thank you for making me a new creature. Thank you that the old is gone and the new is here. I praise you for that miracle in my life. Give me strength through your Holy Spirit to walk in this new way of life. Help me to treat fellow Christian like they are new creations also. Show me the beauty of your ways. Amen."

DAY SIX

"For we are God's handiwork, created in Christ Jesus to do good works, which God prepared in advance for us to do."

Ephesians 2:10

  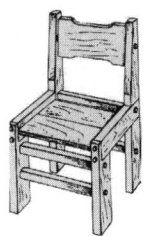

When the carpenter begins his project, he has a plan for what he is going to make. He needs to know the purpose for which the end product will serve. The product is his handiwork. In the picture above the handiwork is the chair and will provide a beautiful seat for someone.

We are God's handiwork. Through Christ Jesus, we are now being formed to do whatever God wants us to do. He already knows our purpose. We are to yield to Him and allow Him to work through us to do good works. Like the chair, we will serve His purpose. Isn't it wonderful to know that God wants to do something incredible through you, his handiwork?

If I live as though Ephesians 2:10 is true, how would I be living?

- First, I would recognize God as the Master Creator, the one in control.

- I must yield to His creating, allowing Him to do what He wants in and through me.

- I will see myself as God sees me, useful to His Kingdom's work.

- I can know that God has a plan for my life and it is way beyond what my mind can comprehend.

- When I look at other Christians, I will see their potential for God's service.

- As led by God, I will serve other Christians.

Consider this prayer:

"Master Creator, thank you for molding me to be who you want me to be. I yield myself to you. Do what you want in and through me. I want to be useful to do good for your Kingdom's sake. Help me as I deal with my Christian brothers and sisters. Let me be a servant to them. Help me see their potential for your service. Amen."

DAY SEVEN

"And by that will, we have been made holy through the sacrifice of the body of Jesus Christ once for all."
Hebrews 10:10

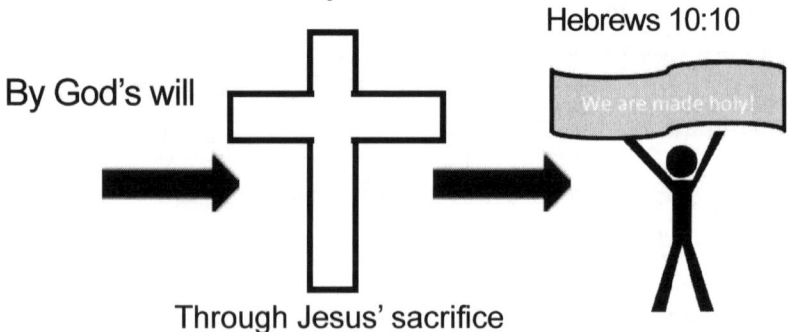

First, God willed it! All that was done for us by Jesus Christ is because of God's grace. It is by God's sovereign will that we have been made holy through Jesus' sacrifice. With Jesus' one-time sacrifice, we are made holy. There is no need for any other sacrifice because Jesus paid it all. Jesus obeyed the will of the Father in giving of Himself to be crucified for our sins.

In the reality of everyday living, where does that leave us? By grace we can live a holy life. Will we be perfect? No. But by God's grace and the help of the Holy Spirit, we can strive to be.

If I live as if Hebrews 10:10 is true, how would I be living?

- Know that Christi died for me.

- His sacrifice was the only one that will ever have to be paid for my sins.

- Through Him I am holy.

- Through Him all Christians are holy.

- By walking with the Holy Spirit daily, I can live in God's holiness. But I cannot do it alone.

- I will treat other Christians with respect and accept that they are, like me, totally dependent on the Holy Spirit to live a Christi-like life.

Consider this prayer:

> "God, thank you for Christ' sacrifice for me. Help me to accept that it is by your grace and His

sacrifice, nothing I have done, that I can live a holy life. Guide me to depend on the Holy Spirit for this walk with you. I want to treat other Christians as you would have me treat them. Help me to see them as you do, holy through Christ. Amen."

DAY EIGHT

Hebrews 2:11 "Both the one who makes people holy and those who are made holy are of the same family. So Jesus is not ashamed to call them brothers and sisters."

Through Jesus, we are a part of a family like none other. We are separated, set apart for purposes beyond worldly desires. Christ makes this possible. We are the recipients of this grace, His holiness. Since we are holy through Christ, we are of the same family. Jesus is not ashamed to call us His brothers and sisters.

Forgiveness Fact or Fiction? - Volume 2 - IDENTITY

If I am living as though Hebrews 2:11 is true, then how would I be living?

- I should live a holy life.

- Know that Jesus and I are in the same family.

- Jesus is not ashamed to call me His brother or sister.

- Realize that other Christians are also a part of this family of God.

- Treat other Christians like I would treat my own family.

- Be thankful that I am a part of God's family and show the world what it means to be a part of His family.

Consider this prayer:

Thank you, God, for allowing me to be a part of your family. Thank you for looking at me, through Jesus, and seeing me as holy. Help me today to walk in the light of your holiness. I cannot do that on my own. I need your Holy Spirit to guide me. Help me to treat other Christians as brothers and sister in Christ. I pray that as I do so, the world will see You in me.

DAY NINE

"Do you not know that your bodies are temples of the Holy Spirit, who is in you, whom you have received from God? You are not your own; you

were bought at a price. Therefore honor God with your bodies."

1 Corinthians 6:19-20

Picture your body as a temple of the Holy Spirit, your own church sanctuary. Would you walk into your church sanctuary and carry out the most grotesque sin that you can think of? These verses tell us that we carry around with us the temple of the Holy Spirit. Everywhere we go and everything we do, in the secret places and in public, represent the Holy Spirit within us. We must honor God with our bodies.

If I am living as though 1 Corinthians 6:19-20 is true, how would I be living?

- Knowing that the Holy Spirit is real and living in me.

- Accepting the guidance of the Holy Spirit in everyday life.

- When I face trials and have to make decisions about honoring God with my body, I will ask the Holy Spirit for help.

- I understand that other Christians deal with issues like mine.
- I will pray for fellow Christians instead of judging them or gossiping.
- Treat my body as God's redemptive creation.

Consider this prayer:

> *Holy Spirit, I give you myself. Forgive me for allowing sin to control my body instead of you. I want to allow you to live freely in my life. When I face temptations and trials today, step in and guide me. As I encounter other Christians, help me to understand their trials and help me to see ways to help them. I give you my body and want to honor you with it. Amen.*

DAY TEN

"For by one sacrifice he has made perfect forever those who are being made holy."
Hebrews 10:14

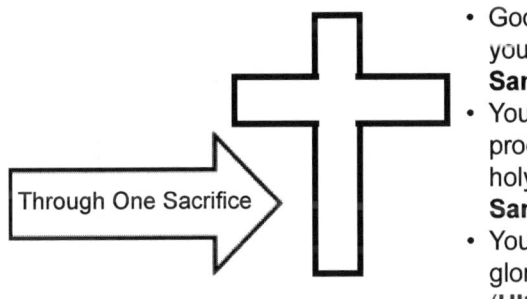

- God has declared you holy. (**Positional Sanctification**)
- You are in the process of becoming holy. (**Experiential Sanctification**)
- You are waiting for glorification in heaven. (**Ultimate Sanctification**)

Through the one sacrifice of Jesus Christ, our sanctification was declared, Positional Sanctification. Each day we are in the process of becoming holy, Experiential Sanctification. One day we will have the Ultimate Sanctification waiting for us in heaven. All of that is given to believers through Jesus' sacrifice on the Cross.

If I live as though Hebrews 10:14 is true, how will I be living?

- Accepting that Jesus' sacrifice was the one sacrifice for all.

- Understanding the three parts of sanctification.
    - Positional Sanctification: Declaration of holiness
    - Experiential Sanctification: The process of holiness.
    - Ultimate Sanctification: Glorification in heaven.

- Know that other Christians are in this same process.

- Live as though I am holy, am experiencing God's perfecting me and one day I will know is complete holiness.

Consider this prayer:

Father, thank you for your sacrifice through your Son Jesus. I know that my life would not be what it is today without Jesus. Help me to allow your Holy Spirit to guide me in a life of holiness as you have declared me holy and are in the process of making me holy. Help me to see other Christians in this light. Guide me to treat them in a holy manner.

CHAPTER FIVE

STAY DEPENDENT ON THE HOLY SPIRIT

God wants us to experience His presence and power through His Holy Spirit every day for the rest of our lives. Ephesians 5:18 says:

> *"Do not get drunk on wine, which leads to debauchery. Instead, be filled with the Spirit."*

God never intended for us to change ourselves. It is God's desire to change us from the inside. When we renew our minds by reading and studying the Word of God, this change occurs. Then we must rely upon the Holy Spirit to help us apply its truths to our lives. We have power over temptation and power to live the kind of life Christ wants us to live every day.

Philip, David and Cody made a last-minute decision to join their church on a mission trip to Mexico. In their rush to make arrangements and pack for their trip, they packed their camera in their suitcase, but forgot to pack the power cord for the camera. When they reached their destination, they realized they could only take a few pictures because the camera had a low battery. They had access to a top-of-the-line camera, but they could not use it because they did not have access to the power cord. In our Christian walk we are sometimes like these guys. We have a relationship with the Almighty God, but we are disconnected because we are not accessing Him through His Holy Spirit.

In John 14:16-18, Jesus comforted His followers with the promise:

> "And I will ask the Father, and he will give you another advocate to help you and be with you forever—the Spirit of truth. The world cannot accept him, because it neither sees him nor knows him. But you know him, for he lives with you and will be in you. I will not leave you as orphans; I will come to you."

The Greek word for "another" means "another just like Me." God sent the Holy Spirit to dwell in us and give us all the spiritual resources we need to live the Christian life successfully.

Who is the Holy Spirit?

The Holy Spirit is God. Jesus is God in a human form and the Holy Spirit is God in spirit form. The Holy Spirit is part of the Trinity: God the Father, God the Son (Jesus), and God the Holy Spirit.

Acts 5:3-4 says:

> "Then Peter said, 'Ananias, how is it that Satan has so filled your heart that you have lied to the Holy Spirit and have kept for yourself some of the money you received for the land."

Didn't it belong to you before it was sold? And after it was sold, wasn't the money at your disposal? What made you think of doing such a thing? You have not lied just to human beings but to God?"

What Role Does the Holy Spirit Play in My Life?

God has given us the Holy Spirit to be the vital source of power for our spiritual lives and to provide everything we need to live the Christian life. The following verses describe the Holy Spirit's role:

- **John 16:7-8:** *"But very truly I tell you, it is for your good that I am going away. Unless I go away, the Advocate will not come to you; but if I go, I will send him to you. When he comes,* **he will convict the world to be in the wrong about sin and righteousness and judgment.***"*

- **John 16:12-14:** *"But when he,* **the Spirit of truth,** *comes,* **he will guide you into all the truth***. He will not speak on his own; he will speak only what he hears, and he will tell you what is yet to come. He will glorify me because it is from me that he will receive what he will make know to you."*

- **Acts 1:8:** ***"But you will receive power when the Holy Spirit comes on you; and you will be my witnesses*** *in Jerusalem, and in all Judea and Samaria, and to the ends of the earth."*

- **Galatians 5:22-23:** *"But the* **fruit of the Spirit is love, joy, peace, forbearance, kindness, goodness, faithfulness, gentleness and self-control.** *Against such things there is no law."*

- **Ephesians 1:13-14:** *"And you also were included in Christ when you heard the message of truth, the gospel of your salvation. When you believed, you were*

Ron Proctor

marked in him with a seal, the promised Holy Spirit, who **is a deposit guaranteeing our inheritance** until the redemption of those who are God's possession—to the praise of his glory."

- **Ephesians 1:17-20:** *"I keep asking that the God of our Lord Jesus Christ, the glorious Father, may give you* **the Spirit of wisdom and revelation***, so that you may know him better. I pray that the eyes of your heart may be enlightened in order that you may know the hope to which he has called you, the riches of his glorious in heritance in his holy people, and his incomparably great* **power** *for us who believe. That power is the same as the* **mighty strength** *he exerted when he raised Christ from the dead and seated him at his right hand in the heavenly realms."*

As you have seen in the verses above, the Holy Spirit plays an active part in your life but only as you learn to walk with Him in control. Look at these illustrations to better understand the difference in a Christian walking through life without the guidance of the Holy Spirit and with His guidance.

Your Experience

Reality of your experience without the Holy Spirit's guidance

Your Experience

According to Galatians 5:22-23, with the Holy Spirit's guidance, your life can look like this.

joy peace **love** patience gentleness **kindness** Satisfied

You experience may tell you that there is no way to know if the Holy Spirit is working in your life, but Galatians 5:22-23 tells you that when you release control of your life to the Holy Spirit, He will produce love, joy, peace, patience, kindness, goodness, faithfulness, gentleness and self-control. Your experience might also say that you do not have the strength to endure the trials you face, but Ephesians 2:16-20 says, that daily you are strengthened through the power of the Holy Spirit, who dwells in you.

What Does It Mean to be Filled with the Holy Spirit?

Paul contrasts a life controlled by the flesh with a life controlled by the Holy Spirit. If you consume too much wine, your attitudes and actions will be affected in a negative way. In contrasts, when the Holy Spirit is in control of your life, you will be able to live in such a way that God's presence will be obvious in your life.

Ephesians 5:18 says:

> "Do not get drunk on wine, which leads to debauchery. Instead, be filled with the Spirit."

The verb phrase that Paul uses: "be filled with the Holy Spirit" means "continually being controlled with the Holy Spirit." The structure of this verb phrase will help you to better understand that Ephesians 5:18 is a command from God that we are to allow the Holy Spirit to control us on a moment by moment basis.

1) It is in the plural form; it is not just for the spiritual elite.

2) It is in the passive voice; it is something the Spirit does to you.

3) It is in the present tense; it is continual and ongoing.

4) It is in the imperative mood; it is a command.

Another way to understand how the Holy Spirit fills our lives is to consider the way a sail functions on a sailboat. As a Christian, you are like a sailboat, and the manifestation of God in your life is equivalent to a breeze. If you choose to open your sail and submit to the control of the wind of the Holy Spirit, then the steady current of air will fill your sail and move you forward. If you do not submit to the control of the wind, then your sailboat will glide pointlessly on the sea.

Being filled with the Spirit does not mean you get more of the Holy Spirit. If you have received God's gift of forgiveness through Jesus, you already have the Holy Spirit living in you through Jesus, you already have the Holy Spirit living in you.

Romans 8:9-11 says:

> "You, however, are not in the realm of the flesh but are in the realm of the Spirit, if indeed the Spirit of God lives in you. And if anyone does not have the Spirit of Christ, they do not belong to Christ. But if Christ is in you, then even though your body is subject to death because of sin, the Spirit gives life because of righteousness. And if the Spirit of him who raised Jesus from the dead is living in you, he who raised Christ from the dead will also give life to your mortal bodies because of his Spirit who lives in you."

THREE SPIRITUAL CONDITIONS

In 1 Corinthians 2:14-3:3, we can see the three spiritual conditions of people represented in these three illustrations.

- The circle represents a person's life.
- The **Cross** presents Christ.
- The **S** represents self.
- The chair represents the control center of a person's life.
- The dots represent the interests, relationships and responsibilities in a person's life.

THE NATURAL-DIRECTED LIFE

Self (**S**) is on the throne

Christ is dethroned and not allowed to direct the life

Interests are directed by self, often resulting in discord and frustration

NATURAL - 1 Corinthians 2:14:

> *"The person without the Spirit does not accept the things that come from the Spirit of God but considers them foolishness, and cannot understand them because they are discerned only through the Spirit."*

This is the non-Christian who does not understand the things of God. They seem foolish to him. The Cross goes outside the circle in the Natural-Directed Life.

THE SPIRITUAL-DIRECTED LIFE

CHRIST is on the throne

Self is yielding to Christ

Interests are directed by Christ, resulting in harmony with God's plan

SPIRITUAL - 1 Corinthians 2:15-16:

> *"The person with the Spirit makes judgments about all things, but such a person is not subject to merely human judgments, for, 'Who has known the mind of the Lord so as to instruct him?' But we have the mind of Christ."*

This is the Christian who is Christ-controlled and empowered by the Spirit of God.

THE FLESHLY-DIRECTED LIFE
Self is on the throne

Interests are directed by self, resulting in discord and frustration

Christ is outside the life

WORDLY OR FLESHLY - 1 Corinthians 3:1-3:

> "Brothers and sisters, I could not address you as people who live by the Spirit but as people whoare still worldly—mere infants in Christ. I gave you milk, not solid food, for you were not ready for it. Indeed, you are still not ready. You are still worldly. For since there is jealousy and quarrelling among you, are you not worldly? Are you not acting like mere humans?"

This is the believer who know Jesus, but is not yielding to God's leadership.The Cross goes outside the circle in the Worldly or Fleshly-Directed life.

    The NATURAL represents someone without the Holy Spirit living in them. The SPIRITUAL represents someone who is controlled by the Holy Spirit. The WORDLY OR FLESHLY represents a Christian who is not submitting to the Holy Spirit. Many Christians are not filled with the Holy Spirit because:

- They do not know. Many Christians do not realize that there are vast resources available to them.

- <u>They do not yield.</u> There is a power struggle going on inside believers. While in their minds they know Jesus is the source of their hope and freedom, in their hearts they maintain control. Romans 12:1-2 says:

    > "Therefore, I urge you, brothers and sisters, in view of God's mercy, to offer your bodies as a living sacrifice, holy and pleasing to God—this is your true and proper worship. Do not conform to the pattern of this world, but be transformed by the renewing of your mind. Then you will be able to test and approve what God's will is—his good, pleasing and perfect will."

- <u>They do not stay in fellowship with Jesus.</u> Many believers receive God's gift of forgiveness through Jesus but then attempt to produce spiritual fruit through their own efforts. Spiritual fruit is a by-product of staying connected to Jesus. John 3:5-8 says:

    > "Jesus answered, 'Very truly I tell you, no one can enter the kingdom of God unless they are born of water and the Spirit. Flesh gives birth to flesh, but the Spirit gives birth to spirit. You should not be surprised at my saying, 'You must be born again.' The wind blows wherever it pleases. You hear its sound, but you cannot tell where it comes from or where it is going. So it is with everyone born of the Spirit.'"

- <u>They do not trust.</u> This lack of trust frequently stems from false beliefs of misconceptions people have about

God. Even though God's love is unconditional, many live in fear of Him and, as a result, do not trust Him. Others believe that God will make their lives miserable if they give Him control. They do not realize that God has good things in store for those who trust in Him.

How Does Someone Experience the Presence and Power of the Holy Spirit?

"We must remember that the filling of the Holy Spirit is not a matter of feeling, but of faith. We may feel strongly the closeness of God when we are filled, or we may not. Instead of trusting in our feelings, we must trust God's Word."

Billy Graham

There are several factors that will prepare your heart for the Spirit's filling.

1. **You must desire to live a life that pleases God.** Matthew 5:6:

    "Wash and make yourselves clean. Take your evil deeds out of my sight; stop doing wrong. Learn to do right; seek justice. Defend the oppressed. Take up the cause of the fatherless; plead the case of the widow."

2. **You must confess any sin that the Holy Spirit brings to mind.** 1 John 1:9:

> *"If we confess our sins, he is faithful and just and will forgive us our sins and purify us from all unrighteousness."*

3. **You must be willing to surrender control of your life to Jesus.** Romans 12:1-2 says:

   > *"Therefore, I urge you, brothers and sisters, in view of God's mercy, to offer your bodies as a living sacrifice, holy and pleasing to God—this is your true and proper worship. Do not conform to the pattern of this world, but be transformed by the renewing of your mind. Then you will be able to test and approve what God's will is—his good, pleasing and perfect will."*

The World, the Flesh and the Devil say:

The Bible says:

| Live by your own rules ... Do what you want to do ... Please yourself and others ... Look to the world for advice | Be a living sacrifice ... Live holy and pleasing to God ... Worship Him ... Don't conform to the world ... Be transformed ... Renew your mind |

4. **You must, by faith, trust the Holy Spirit to fill you according to:**

   - God's command that you be filled with His Spirit. Ephesians 5:18:

     > *"Do not get drunk on wine, which leads to debauchery. Instead, be filled with the Spirit."*

- God's promise that He will answer when you pray according to His will. 1 John 5:14-15:

"This is the confidence we have in approaching God: that if we ask anything according to his will, he hears us. And if we know that he hears us—whatever we ask—we know that we have what we asked of him."

Being filled with the Holy Spirit is something that God desires for every believer. Even if you learn to be filled with the Holy Spirit and you ask God to fill you with His Spirit on a daily basis, you will still encounter conflict. If you are not prepared for spiritual conflict, you will not be prepared to handle it. By faith, choose to believe that God wants you to experience His presence and power every day through His Holy Spirit. In order for the Holy Spirit to demonstrate His power in a life, every believer must take responsibility for yielding to the Holy Spirit's control.

God wants every Christian to experience His presence and power through the Holy Spirit every day for the rest of our lives!

God never intended for us to change ourselves. It is God's desire to change us from the inside. This change occurs when we renew our minds by reading and studying the Word of God. Then we must rely upon the Holy Spirit to help us apply its truths to our lives. We have power over temptation and power to live the kind of life Christ wants us to live every day.

When a Christian chooses to walk under the control of the Holy Spirit they face conflict. That conflict comes from the adversary, Satan. He is our enemy and he does not want us to walk under the control of the Holy Spirit. Sometimes Christians fail to live under the control of the Holy Spirit and therefore, have difficulty experiencing the type of life that Jesus died for on the Cross at Calvary.

CHANGE OCCURS WHEN THE WORD OF GOD BECOMES EMPOWERED BY THE SPIRIT OF GOD.

HOW CAN A CHRISTIAN BE PREPARED FOR SPIRITUAL CONFLICT?

You will discover that even after you give control of your life to God and ask Him to fill you with His Holy Spirit, you will still encounter conflict from the world, your flesh and the devil. It is important to remember that soldiers are sometimes mortally wounded when they forget they are in a war.

DO NOT UNDERESTIMATE THE CONFLICT THAT EXISTS BETWEEN YOU & SATAN!

As a Christian, you still need to be ready for the three sources of opposition that can impede your walk with Christ:

OPPOSITION #1: THE WORLD

*"Do not love the **world** nor the things in the **world**. If anyone loves the **world**, the love of the Father is not in him. For all that is in the **world**, the lust of the flesh and the lust of the eyes and the boastful pride of life, is not from the Father,*

*but is from the **world**. The **world** is passing away, and also its lusts; but the one who does the will of God lives forever."*
1 John 2 15-17

If we are not careful, it is easy for LIFE to squeeze us into following what the world is doing. Consider this illustration. Joe has just left a defensive driving course. After hearing all the statistics concerning speeding and fatal car wrecks, he has committed to never speed again. Joe arranged to meet some friends at a restaurant on the other side of town. To get to the restaurant and take the proper exit, Joe must cross all four lanes on the freeway. To do that, he must keep up with the flow of traffic. The speed limit is 60 miles per hour, yet the other cars are travelling at a pace of 75 miles per hour. As the traffic speeds by Joe finds himself under tremendous pressure to stay in the flow of traffic meaning going their speed instead of obeying the traffic laws.

The world's system works the same way. We try to follow the person of Jesus Christ and the world is constantly squeezing us into the going the opposite direction.

Romans 12:2 says:

"Do not conform to the pattern of this world, but be transformed by the renewing of your mind. Then you will be able to test and approve what God's will is—his good, pleasing and perfect will."

J. B. Phillips paraphrased this as "Stop letting the world squeeze you into its mold." This means that you should not let the world impact your thinking or how you behave. The pressure of the traffic flow will continue to push and PUSH and **PUSH**! What is happening in the Christian community today is very similar. We are being pressured to conform to the world. That constant pressure pushes and **PUSHES** and **PUSHES** us to conform to the world's way of thinking.

OPPOSITION #2: THE FLESH

Galatians 5:16-23 says that if we walk by the Spirit we will NOT carry out the desire of the flesh.
What happens if we don't walk with the Spirit but walk in the flesh?

- The flesh is against the Spirit, total opposition.

- Fleshly deeds will be evident in your life (immorality, impurity, sensuality, idolatry, sorcery, enmities, strife, jealousy, outburst of anger, disputes, dissensions, factions, envying, drunkenness, carousing).

What happens if we walk in the Spirit and not in the flesh?

- Fruit of the Spirit will be present in our lives (love, joy, peace, patience, kindness, goodness, faithfulness, gentleness, self-control).

OPPOSITION #3 SATAN

Satan uses the world's system and our flesh against us by tempting us to follow the world's system and what our flesh desires to do. When Peter tried to dissuade Jesus from going to the Cross, Jesus rebuked him. He said, "Get behind me, Satan!" Jesus was aware that attacks came from all sides, even from within His own circle of followers.

The following passages tell us just how the devil operates:

HE IS SCHEMING.

> "Put on the full armor of God, so that you can take your stand against the devil's schemes."
> Ephesians 6:11

HE IS OUR ENEMY, SEEKING TO KILL.

> "Be alert and of sober mind. Your enemy the devil prowls around like a roaring lion looking for someone to devour."
> 1 Peter 5:8

HE LEADS THE WHOLE WORLD ASTRAY AND ACCUSES THE BELIEVERS.

> "The great dragon was hurled down—that ancient serpent called the devil, or Satan, who leads the whole world astray. He was hurled to the earth, and his angels with him. Then I heard a loud voice in heaven say: 'Now have come the salvation and the power and the kingdom of our God, and the authority of his Messiah. For the accuser of our brothers and sisters, who accuse them before our God day and night, has been hurled down."
> Revelations 12:9-10

If you have ever been on a safari and encountered a lion in the wild, it can be a terrifying experience. A pack of lions will congregate around a watering hole, but it is not uncommon for a male lion to fall asleep several yards away from the rest of the pack. You could even get close enough to see its teeth. As long as the lion is asleep you will not be in danger. At the same time, if you get close enough to one of the females who is awake and at the watering hole, you could be in grave danger. The sleeping lion will not bother you, but the lion that is hungry, the one that is looking for food, is dangerous.

> **If you live in Africa, you must understand the ways of the lion. If you are going to walk under the power of the Holy Spirit, you must know the ways of the lion, SATAN.**

Satan is out to kill you, steal from you and destroy you. He lies. He tricks His very name means "tripper." He tries to keep you from walking under the control of God's Spirit. Remember, if you are going to operate in the spiritual realm, you have to understand the ways of the lion.

WHAT ARE MY RESOURCES AS A CHILD OF GOD?

When you became a Christian, God adopted you into His own family. You became one of His children.

> *"Yet to all who did receive him, to those who believed in his name, he gave right to become children of God."*
>
> John 1:12

Once you belong to Christ, God's limitless resources are available to you. These resources are described in God's Word. The more you read and study the Bible, the

more you will understand your position in God's family and how you can accept His power every day.
Here are a few of the resources available to Christians as described in these passages:

1. Power to be a witness for Christ.

> "But you will receive power when the Holy Spirit comes on you; and you will be my witnesses in Jerusalem, and in all Judea and Samaria, and to the ends of the earth."
> Acts 1:8

2. Holy and blameless in his sight.

> "For he chose us in him before the creation of the world to be holy and blameless in his sight."
> Ephesians 1:4

3. Redemption and forgiveness of sin.

> "In him we have redemption through his blood, the forgiveness of sins, in accordance with the riches of God's grace."
> Ephesians 1:7

4. The Holy Spirit.

> "When you believed, you were marked in him with a seal, the promised Holy Spirit, who is a deposit guaranteeing our inheritance until the redemption of those who are God's possession—
> to the praise of his glory."
> Ephesians 1:13b-14

5. Wisdom and revelation.

> *"I keep asking that the God of our Lord Jesus Christ, the glorious Father, may give you the Spirit of wisdom and revelation, so that you may know him better."*
> Ephesians 1:17

6. His great power.

> *"And his incomparably great power for us who believe."*
> Ephesians 1:19a

7. The full armor of God.

> *"Stand firm then, with the belt of truth buckled around your waist, with the breastplate of righteousness in place, and with your feet fitted with the readiness that comes from the gospel of peace. In addition to all this, take up the shield of faith, with which you can extinguish all the flaming arrows of the evil one. Take the helmet of salvation and the sword of the Spirit, which is the word of God."*
> Ephesians 6:14-17

8. God's Holy Word.

> *"For the word of God is alive and active. Sharper than any double-edged sword, it penetrates even to dividing soul and spirit, joints and marrow; it judges the thoughts and attitudes of the heart."*
> Hebrews 4:12

As we allow ourselves to be filled with the Holy Spirit, the more we utilize the resources that are available to us as children of God. Then, our lives will be productive, and our ministries will be effective because His Spirit is applying His Word in our lives. God does not force us to obey Him; however, the more we understand what He has given us, the more we desire to do His will.

YOUR LIFE TODAY

The essence of the Christian life is what God does in you and through you!

We are empowered by the Holy Spirit through faith alone. The following prayer is one way to express your faith that God will fill you with His Spirit:

Dear Jesus, I need You. I acknowledge that I have been directing my own life and that, as a result, I have sinned against You. I thank You that you have forgiven my sins through Christ's death on the Cross. I now invite Your Holy Spirit to take His place again on the throne of my life. Fill me with the Holy Spirit as You have commanded me to be filled and as You promised in Your Word that You would do if I asked in faith. As an expression of my faith, I thank You for directing my life and for filling me with the Holy Spirit.

HOW DO I MAINTAIN THE FILLING OF THE SPIRIT?

Spiritual Breathing is a simple exercise that maintains the filling of the Holy Spirit. It involves two parts: exhaling and inhaling. Spiritual breathing becomes a daily discipline for every Child of God.

EXHALE

When you become aware of sin in your life, confess it immediately and accept God's forgiveness

INHALE:

Surrender the control of your life to Jesus and, by faith, trust that the Holy Spirit empowers you.

Forgiveness Fact or Fiction? - Volume 2 - IDENTITY

The Apostle Paul frequently emphasized the empowering of the Holy Spirit in his letters to the early churches. Ephesians 3:14-21 is one of Paul's prayers for the Ephesians Christians.

> *"For this reason I kneel before the Father, from whom His whole family in heaven and on earth derives its name. I pray that out of his glorious riches He may strengthen you with power through his Spirit in your inner being, so that Christ may dwell in your hearts through faith. And I pray that you, being rooted and established in love, may have power, together with all the saints, to grasp how wide and long and high and deep is the love of Christ, and to know this love that surpasses knowledge—that you may be filled to the measure of all the fullness of God. Now to Him who is able to do immeasurably more than all we ask or imagine, according to His power that is at work within us, to Him be glory in the church and in Christ Jesus throughout all generations,*
> *for ever and ever! Amen."*

God wants all Christians to experience His presence and power every day through His Holy spirit. Every day, it is each Christian's responsibility to yield control of his life to Him in order for Him to demonstrate His power.

About the Author

Ron Proctor was educated at Dallas Baptist University, Southwestern Baptist theological Seminary, and Dallas Theological Seminary. He has been teaching and mentoring at Dallas Baptist University for many years. He is the husband of Della, the father of Deborah, Josh, and Kelly (daughter-in-law), and grandfather of nine.